Unlock the AI Revolution

A Step-by-Step Journey
For Beginners Over 59

Mark T. Matthew

Unlock the AI Revolution

A Step-by-Step Journey For Beginners Over 59

Published by: Mark T. Matthew

Your honest feedback is invaluable! Please consider leaving a review on Amazon to share your thoughts.

Table of Contents

Chapter 1

The Golden Chapter

This might be the best and most important chapter in this book, which is why I called it the golden chapter. And why do I call it the golden chapter? Because it is simple, objective, and straight; and it can be considered a synthesis of what artificial intelligence is. It does not contain complicated technical information, but sufficient and necessary information for the reader to be able, on their own, to effectively use AI, making it a powerful tool to be incorporated into daily life.

Often, the best is saved for last. But I decided to reverse that order. The best is here, and the reader will most likely consult the pages to come frequently, as this is what this chapter ambitiously aims to be: a simple reference on the potential of AI.

In fact, this is a chapter for AI beginners of all ages. It is a chapter with basic, but nonetheless fundamental, information; without which it is impossible to advance.

So, the reader asks: why does the book's title refer to beginners over 59 years old? Because, in general, people in this age range feel uncomfortable with new technologies and believe they are not capable of keeping up with the changes because they are too complicated. This chapter, in particular, aims to debunk these false notions and encourage people over 59 to overcome this discomfort and engage, without fear, in mastering AI. Yes! That's a promise! By reading the information contained in this chapter alone, the reader will have enough information to explore AI in various ways.

I won't go into historical details regarding the revolutions that humanity has already gone through. We have already faced the industrial revolution, the electricity revolution, the communications revolution, the internet revolution, the smartphone revolution, and the social media revolution, just to mention the most impactful ones. All these revolutions had the power to radically change people's way of life. New habits, new jobs, new companies, new products, conveniences, and much wealth were created. However, I have no hesitation in stating that AI is the greatest of all the technological revolutions we have known. Mistake! The changes that AI will make – or rather, already makes – are overwhelmingly greater than all other revolutions combined. In a few years, many of the services offered by companies will be entirely based on AI.

So, enough talk! As Socrates once said to Gorgias: "Let us leave the abundance of words for another occasion; now, let us seek to understand each other clearly, by questioning and answering."

In simple terms, what is AI?
If I were allowed to define AI in one word, I would say: **Magic**.

Going a little further, AI can be considered a supercomputer that has learned and absorbed all human knowledge, in all areas, and interacts as if it were indeed a human, capable of performing various tasks: texts, poems, music, chats, books, images, videos, and much more.

What does the term generative AI mean?
Generative AI, or generative Artificial Intelligence, refers to a type of artificial intelligence that has the ability to create new content. Unlike other types of AI that focus on analyzing existing data, classifying information, or making predictions, generative AI goes further, producing something original.

Imagine an artist who learned to paint by observing

thousands of paintings. Generative AI works similarly: it is trained with a large volume of data (texts, images, audios, videos, etc.) and, from this learning, it can generate new examples that follow the learned patterns but are not copies of the original data.

Practical examples of generative AI:
- **Text**: Writing poems, articles, scripts, emails, summaries, translations, and even programming code.
- **Images**: Creating realistic photos, paintings, illustrations, product designs, and even generating variations of an existing image.
- **Audio**: Composing music, generating sound effects, dubbing videos, and synthesizing voices.
- **Video**: Creating animations, generating realistic scenes, and editing videos.

In which areas does generative AI have the potential to operate?
- **Content creation:** Marketing, advertising, design, entertainment, and journalism.
- **Health:** Developing new medications, medical diagnosis, and creating personalized prostheses.
- **Engineering and design:** Creating prototypes, optimizing projects, and developing new materials.
- **Education:** Creating personalized teaching

materials and interactive learning experiences.

- **Business:** Automating repetitive tasks, analyzing large volumes of data to predict market trends and assisting in strategic decision-making.
- **Mobility:** Autonomous vehicles, making transportation safer, more efficient, and accessible. Route and traffic optimization: analyzing real-time traffic data to optimize routes and reduce congestion.
- **Environment:** Environmental monitoring: analyzing data to monitor deforestation, pollution, and other environmental issues. Natural disaster prediction.
- **Accessibility:** AI develops solutions for people with disabilities, such as screen readers and voice recognition software.

How do I get started with AI?

There are several AI tools available on the market, each with its strengths and specific characteristics. Choosing the best tool depends on your needs and objectives. Below, I list some of the main alternatives, categorizing them for better understanding:

Large Language Models (LLMs) with multimodal capabilities (text, image, code, etc.):

- **Claude (Anthropic):** Developed by Anthropic,

Claude stands out for its safety and reliability, seeking to avoid incorrect answers and biases. It is effective in tasks such as complex data analysis, creative content generation, and conversation. Claude 2, the latest version, demonstrates improvements over previous versions.

- **GPT-4 (OpenAI):** The model behind ChatGPT Plus, GPT-4 is one of the most advanced LLMs available. It has a high capacity for text comprehension and generation, in addition to handling images (in beta). It is widely used for content creation, chatbots, text summarization, and much more.

- **PaLM 2 (Google):** Although Gemini is Google's latest model, PaLM 2 is still a powerful option, with good performance in various natural language tasks, including translation, summarization, and code generation. It serves as the basis for Google Bard.

- **Gemini (Google):** Gemini, Google's latest family of artificial intelligence (AI) models, is capable of a wide range of tasks, combining the resources of large language models with advanced reasoning and multimodality capabilities. In simple terms, Gemini understands and operates with different types of information, such as text, code, images, audio, and video.

- **Microsoft Copilot:** Microsoft Copilot is a suite of AI tools that integrates large language models with the Microsoft ecosystem, enhancing productivity across various applications like Word, Excel, PowerPoint, and more. In simple terms, Copilot assists users with tasks ranging from generating text and code to creating presentations and analyzing data, by understanding and working with different forms of information within the Microsoft environment.

Chatbot and conversation-focused platforms.
- **ChatGPT (OpenAI)**: The free version of ChatGPT, based on GPT-3.5, offers an excellent introduction to language models. It is useful for generating text, answering questions, and brainstorming ideas, although it may have some limitations compared to GPT-4.
- **Google Bard (Google):** Using PaLM 2, Bard seeks to provide informative and comprehensive answers, with access to web information. It is a good option for research, brainstorming, and text generation.
- **Character.AI:** Focused on creating virtual characters with distinct personalities, Character.AI allows for fun and creative interactions.

Tools with specialized features

- **TextCortex:** In addition to being an alternative to Gemini with real-time web browsing, TextCortex offers file uploading and style customization features, allowing you to work with your own data.
- **Writesonic:** Focused on creating marketing content, Writesonic offers tools to generate texts for ads, blog posts, product descriptions, and other materials.
- **Jasper:** Similar to Writesonic, Jasper offers resources for creating marketing content and also integrates with other tools.

Further relevant options:

- **Perplexity AI:** Focused on providing answers with citations and sources, Perplexity AI is useful for research and searching for reliable information.
- **You.com:** A search engine that uses AI to provide direct and concise answers, in addition to offering chat features.

Important Considerations:

- **Availability and pricing:** Some tools offer free versions with limited features, while others require paid subscriptions.
- **Specific uses:** Each tool may be more suitable for certain types of tasks. Evaluate your specific needs

before choosing.
- **Security and privacy practices:** Consider the privacy and security policies of each platform, especially when dealing with sensitive data.

What is an LLM?
LLM stands for Large Language Model and is designed to understand, generate, and manipulate human language. They are "large" because they are trained on massive amounts of text and code data, which allows them to learn complex patterns in language.

What are the applications of LLMs?
The applications are diverse. Here are some:
- **Text generation:** Writing articles, emails, poems, scripts, etc.
- **Automatic translation:** Translating text from one language to another.
- **Chatbots and virtual assistants:** Creating natural conversations with users.
- **Text summarization:** Condensing large amounts of text into concise summaries.
- **Sentiment analysis:** Determining the emotional tone of a text.
- **Code generation:** Writing code in various programming languages.
- **Question answering:** Answering questions

informatively and comprehensively.

How to get started with Gemini (Google AI)?

Gemini can be accessed in various ways, but we will focus on access with desktop computers.

Via browser:

- Go to the website: gemini.google.com
- Log in with your Google account
- Start typing your commands (prompts) and press "Send".

What does the Gemini screen look like?

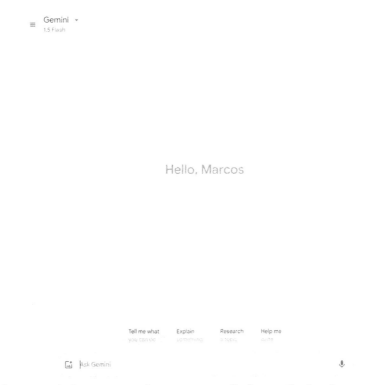

The Gemini screen, when accessed through the browser, has the following characteristics:

- **Clean and conversation-focused interface:** The design is minimalist, with the main focus on the text box where you enter your prompts and the area where Gemini's responses are displayed.
- **Prompt text box:** Located at the bottom of the screen, this is where you type your questions, commands, or requests for the AI.
- **Response display area:** Above the text box,

Gemini's responses appear in text format and may also include other elements, such as:

- ○ **Image thumbnails with links to sources:** If the response includes visual information from the web, Gemini displays an image thumbnail with the source and a direct link to the original page.
- ○ **Google button:** To check the information in Gemini's response using Google Search, there is a dedicated button.

- **Top bar (or tab in the Google app):** Depending on whether you access it through the browser or the Google app, there will be a way to switch between traditional Search and Gemini. In the Google app, a tab at the top allows this switching.
- **Conversation history:** Your previous conversations with Gemini are saved and can be accessed later. In the Google app, these conversations can be found in "Gemini app activity".

The Gemini screen prioritizes conversational interaction, with a simple and direct interface that facilitates sending prompts and viewing responses.

What are prompts?

In the context of large language models (LLMs) like Gemini, a prompt is the initial input you provide to the model to generate a response or perform a specific task. In other words, it's the command or instruction you give to the AI.

Think of a prompt as a question, a request, or a context that you offer to the model to direct its output. The quality of the prompt directly influences the quality of the AI-generated response.

What are the types of prompts?

There are several types of prompts, depending on the task you want the AI to perform:

- **Questions**: The most common type of prompt. You ask a direct question and expect an informative answer.
  - **Example**: "What is the capital of France?"
- **Instructions:** You provide a clear instruction about what the AI should do.
  - **Example:** "Write a poem about nature."
- **Context and request:** You provide a context and then request a specific action.
  - **Example:** "Here is an excerpt from a book: 'Once upon a time...'. Continue the story."
- **Examples (few-shot learning):** You provide some examples of desired inputs and outputs so

that the AI learns the pattern and generates new outputs based on that pattern.

- **Example:** "Translate to French: 'Hello' -> 'Bonjour', 'How are you?' -> 'Comment allez-vous?', 'Thank you' -> ... (the AI should complete with 'Merci')"

- **Creative prompts:** You ask the AI to create something original, such as a story, a song, or a script.

- **Example:** "Create a science fiction story about time travel."

How to create good prompts?

Creating good prompts is crucial for getting the best results from LLMs. Here are some tips:

- **Be clear and specific:** The more specific your prompt, the more targeted the AI's response will be. Avoid ambiguities and be as precise as possible.

- **Provide context:** If necessary, provide additional context to help the AI better understand your request.

- **Use relevant keywords:** Including relevant keywords can help the AI generate a more accurate response.

- **Try different formulations:** If you are not satisfied with the first response, try rephrasing the prompt in different ways.

- **Consider the tone and style:** You can specify the desired tone and style for the response, such as formal, informal, humorous, etc.
- **Break down complex tasks into smaller prompts:** For more complex tasks, it can be helpful to break them down into smaller, sequential prompts.

What would a practical example look like?

Scenario 1: Writing a letter:
Bad Prompt: "Write a text to the CEO about a product I invented."
It's bad because it's *insufficiently specific* for an AI to produce a truly useful result. It lacks crucial context, leading to a generic or potentially irrelevant output.
Here's why it's a weak prompt:

- **No information about the product:** The AI has no idea what the product is, its features, its benefits, or its target market. This makes it impossible to write a compelling or informative message.
- **No purpose for the text:** Is the text meant to:
  - Introduce the product for the first time?
  - Request a meeting to discuss it further?
  - Provide a brief update on its development?
  - Seek funding or approval? The purpose

drastically changes the content and tone of the text.

- **No context about the relationship with the CEO:** Is this person a close colleague, someone the inventor has never met, or someone in between? This affects the level of formality and the approach.
- **No desired tone or style:** Should the text be formal, informal, enthusiastic, concise, detailed, etc.?

Good Prompt: "Develop a persuasive business proposal introduction for the CEO of [Company X], a leading force in the [Market Y] sector. My novel product addresses a critical unmet need in this market, promising significant revenue growth and profitability. This introduction should highlight the synergy between my product and [Company X]'s existing infrastructure and market reach, emphasizing the potential for a highly successful partnership. Express my eagerness to explore this opportunity further in a formal and respectful manner."

Scenario 2: Creating an image of a cat.
Bad Prompt: "Draw a cat"

- Why it's bad: This is far too vague. The AI has no idea what kind of cat, what pose, what setting, or what style you want. You could get anything from a cartoon cat to a photorealistic cat, a kitten, an adult cat, a cat sleeping, a cat hunting, etc. It's like asking a painter to "paint a thing."

Good Prompt: "Create a fluffy ginger tabby cat, curled up asleep on a cozy blue armchair, soft lighting, photorealistic style"

- Why it's good: This prompt provides much more detail:
    - Specific breed/type: "ginger tabby" gives the AI a clear idea of the cat's appearance.
    - Action/pose: "curled up asleep" specifies what the cat is doing.
    - Setting/environment: "on a cozy blue armchair" provides context and background.
    - Lighting: "soft lighting" influences the mood and atmosphere.
    - Style: "photorealistic style" tells the AI to create a realistic image, not a cartoon or painting.

Scenario 3: Creating an image of a garden.

Bad Prompt: "Give an image of a garden"

- Why it's bad: Again, extremely vague. The AI could generate anything from a desert cactus garden to a formal French garden, a vegetable garden, a flower garden, etc.

Good Prompt: "Create a vibrant English cottage garden in full bloom, overflowing with colorful flowers like roses, lavender, and foxgloves, a winding stone path, sunny afternoon light, impressionist painting style"

- Why it's good: This prompt is much more descriptive:
    - Type of garden: "English cottage garden" gives a specific style.
    - Specific elements: "colorful flowers like roses, lavender, and foxgloves" tells the AI what to include.
    - Features: "a winding stone path" adds detail to the scene.
    - Time of day/lighting: "sunny afternoon light" sets the mood.
    - Artistic style: "impressionist painting style" tells the AI to create an image in the style of impressionist art.

Key takeaways for you:
- **Be specific:** The more details you provide, the better the results will be.
- **Use descriptive language:** Use adjectives and adverbs to paint a picture with words.
- **Consider the style:** Specify whether you want a photo, a painting, a drawing, or a specific artistic style.
- **Experiment:** Try different prompts and see what works best.

Scenario 4: Let's say you're planning a trip to Italy.
Bad Prompt: "Italy trip"

- Why it's bad: This is incredibly vague. It gives the AI no information about what you want to know. Do you want to know about:
  - Where to go in Italy?
  - When to go?
  - What to see and do?
  - How much it will cost?
  - What kind of trip (relaxing, adventurous, cultural)?
  - What your interests are (art, food, history)?
  - How long you're going for?

The AI might give you very general information about Italy, which isn't helpful for planning a specific trip.

Good Prompt: "I'm planning a 10-day trip to Italy in October with my partner. We're interested in art, history, and good food. We'd like to visit Rome and Florence, but we're open to other suggestions. We prefer a moderate pace with a mix of sightseeing and relaxation. Can you suggest a possible itinerary, including key attractions, estimated costs, and transportation options between cities?"

- Why it's good: This prompt provides much more detail:

- Duration: "10-day trip"
- Time of year: "in October"
- Travel companions: "with my partner"
- Interests: "art, history, and good food"
- Desired destinations: "Rome and Florence"
- Flexibility: "open to other suggestions"
- Pace of travel: "moderate pace with a mix of sightseeing and relaxation"
- Specific request: "suggest a possible itinerary, including key attractions, estimated costs, and transportation options between cities"

With this detailed prompt, the AI can provide a much more relevant and useful response, such as:

- A day-by-day itinerary suggestion.
- Recommendations for specific museums, historical sites, and restaurants.
- Information on train travel between Rome and Florence.
- A rough estimate of costs for accommodation, food, and activities.

The key takeaway is that the more details you provide in your prompt, the more relevant and helpful the AI's response will be. Think about all the aspects of your trip and include them in your prompt to get the best results.

In summary, prompts are the key to interacting effectively with LLMs. Mastering the art of creating good prompts allows you to make the most of the potential of these powerful AI tools. The more specific and detailed the instructions, the better the results will be.

Conclusion

The "Golden Chapter" provides an accessible and comprehensive introduction to AI, with a special focus on generative AI and its practical applications. By presenting various tools and detailing the concept of "prompts," the chapter empowers the reader to begin actively exploring the world of AI. The emphasis on demystifying the technology and encouraging beginners, especially those over 59, is an important differentiator. The chapter emphasizes the importance of clarity and specificity in creating prompts, demonstrating that the quality of interaction with AI depends on the quality of the instructions provided. In short, the chapter serves as a practical and inspiring guide for anyone interested in understanding and using AI.

The following table summarizes some of the AI available, (some of them are discussed in this book) serving as a quick reference for consultation.

Unlock The AI Revolution:
A Step-by-Step Journey for Beginners Over 59

The Golden Table

Theme	Tool
AI with multimodal capabilities (text, image, code, etc.):	Claude, GPT-4, PaLM 2, Gemini, Copilot
Chatbot & conversation-focused platforms.	ChatGPT, Google Bard, Character.AI
Tools with specialized features	TextCortex, Writesonic, Jasper, Perplexity AI, You.com
Write Assistants	Grammarly, Notion AI, Otter.ai, ChatGPT, Copy.ai, Writesonic
Apps for Fitness, Mental Health	MyFitnessPal, Headspace, Sleep Tracking
AI Image Creation	MidJourney, DALLE-E, DeepArt, artistly.ai , Talkingphotos.ai,
AI-Powered Learning	Duolingo, Coursera
Personal Finance Aps	Mint, Acorns, YNAB
Stock Analysis Tools	Trade Ideas, Zacks, Alpha Vantage
Create AI videos	Synthesia, Deepbrain AI, Runway,Fliki, Pictory, Luma Labs Dream Machine
AI-Powered Learning	Duolingo, Coursera
Personal Finance Aps	Mint, Acorns, YNAB
Financial Planning	Betterment, Wealthfront
Personal Productivity	RescueTime, Trello, Todoist
Automating Repetitive Test	Zapier, IFTTT
Career Development	Rezi, Jobscan, ZipRecruiter
Skill Develpment	Coursera, Udemy
Art & Music	DALLE-E, DeepArt, Aiva
Brainstrom Ideas & Inspiration	BuzzSumo, Jarvis, Lately AI, Amper Music

Chapter 2

Introduction to AI

What is AI?

Artificial Intelligence (AI) refers to the capability of a machine to imitate intelligent human behavior. Essentially, AI involves creating algorithms and systems that allow computers to perform tasks that typically require human intelligence, such as understanding language, recognizing patterns, making decisions, and even learning from experience.

At its core, AI seeks to simulate cognitive functions like **learning**, **reasoning**, and **problem-solving**. For example, voice assistants like **Siri** and **Alexa** use AI to understand spoken commands and respond appropriately. Similarly, AI is used in self-driving cars to make decisions based on sensor data from the environment.

While **AI**, **Machine Learning (ML)**, and **Deep Learning (DL)** are often used interchangeably, they represent different levels of sophistication:

- **Artificial Intelligence (AI):**
  AI is the broader concept of creating machines that can mimic intelligent human behavior. It encompasses all technologies that enable machines to perform tasks normally requiring human intelligence.
- **Machine Learning (ML):**
  ML is a subset of AI that focuses on algorithms that allow machines to learn from data and improve over time without being explicitly programmed. ML models are trained on data and they use statistical methods to find patterns and make predictions.
- **Deep Learning (DL):**
  DL is a subset of Machine Learning that uses artificial neural networks (inspired by the human brain) to process data in layers. Deep learning models are especially effective for tasks like image recognition, natural language processing, and speech recognition. These models require large amounts of data and computational power to train but can produce highly accurate results.

In summary:
- **AI** is the broad goal of autonomous machine intelligence.

- **ML** is a technique for achieving AI by allowing machines to learn from data.
- **DL** is a more advanced technique within ML that uses neural networks to handle complex tasks.

Brief History of AI: How It Started and Where It Is Now

AI has a rich and evolving history. Here's a brief timeline:

1. 1950s - The Birth of AI:

The concept of AI was first introduced in the 1950s by pioneers like **Alan Turing**, who proposed the **Turing Test** as a way to measure machine intelligence. **John McCarthy**, who coined the term **"Artificial Intelligence"**, organized the famous **Dartmouth Conference** in 1956, which is considered the official birth of AI as a field of study.

2. 1960s-1970s - Early AI Programs:

The early years of AI research focused on symbolic reasoning and problem-solving. Programs like **ELIZA** (a chatbot) and **SHRDLU** (a natural language processing program) were created, which could perform tasks like answering questions or manipulating objects in a virtual world.

3. 1980s - The Rise of Expert Systems:

AI research saw a boom in the 1980s with the development of **expert systems**, which used rule-based reasoning to simulate decision-making in specific domains, such as medical diagnosis and finance.

4. 1990s - Machine Learning Emerges:

In the 1990s, researchers began to focus on **Machine Learning**, where systems learn from data rather than relying on hard-coded rules. Notable achievements include **IBM's Deep Blue**, which defeated the world chess champion **Garry Kasparov** in 1997.

5. 2000s - Big Data and Computational Power:

The 2000s saw rapid advances in AI, fueled by the availability of **big data** and increased **computational power**. This era also marked the rise of **AI applications** in business, such as recommendation systems and predictive analytics.

6. 2010s - The Deep Learning Revolution:

The 2010s witnessed breakthroughs in **Deep Learning**, particularly with the development of **neural networks** that could recognize objects in images, understand speech, and even generate text. The success of deep learning models like **AlphaGo** (developed by **DeepMind**) and **GPT-3** (a natural language model by OpenAI) demonstrated the enormous potential of AI in a variety of fields.

7. 2020s - AI in Everyday Life:
Today, AI is becoming ubiquitous in everyday life, from **voice assistants** like Siri to **AI-powered healthcare systems**, **autonomous vehicles**, and **personalized marketing**. AI is transforming industries like healthcare, finance, entertainment, and education, and its influence is expected to grow exponentially in the coming years.

The Growing Influence of AI in Various Industries

AI is revolutionizing industries across the globe, with profound impacts on:

- **Healthcare**: AI is transforming diagnostics, drug discovery, personalized medicine, and patient care. AI models can analyze medical images (e.g., **X-rays**, **MRIs**) to detect diseases like cancer earlier and more accurately than human doctors.
- **Finance**: AI is used in algorithmic trading, fraud detection, credit scoring, and risk management. AI-powered systems can analyze vast amounts of financial data and make real-time decisions.
- **Entertainment**: Streaming services like **Netflix** and **Spotify** use AI to recommend movies, TV shows, and music based on user preferences. AI is

also used in video game design, film production, and content creation.

- **Manufacturing**: AI-driven automation, predictive maintenance, and quality control are optimizing production lines and reducing operational costs.
- **Retail**: AI is used in customer service (e.g., chatbots), inventory management, personalized recommendations, and demand forecasting.

AI's influence is only expected to grow, as more industries realize its potential to improve efficiency, enhance customer experiences, and enable new innovations.

Why AI Matters Today?

The Benefits of AI in Daily Life

AI is already integrated into our daily lives, often in ways we don't even notice. Some of the benefits include:

- **Automation**: AI automates repetitive tasks, saving time and reducing human error. For example, AI handles customer service inquiries via chatbots and automates tasks in industries like manufacturing and logistics.
- **Personalization**: - AI can tailor experiences to individual users. For instance, recommendation systems on platforms like **Amazon, Netflix**, and

YouTube suggest content based on your preferences, making it easier to find relevant products, movies, or videos.
- **Convenience**: AI-powered assistants like **Google Assistant** and **Siri** help us manage daily tasks like setting reminders, sending texts, or answering questions, making our lives more efficient.
- **Improved Decision-Making**: AI systems analyze large amounts of data and provide insights that can help people make better decisions, whether in healthcare, finance, or marketing.

How AI Shapes the Future of Work, Learning, and Personal Development
- **Work**: AI is reshaping the workplace by automating routine tasks, allowing workers to focus on more strategic and creative tasks. It also enables **remote work**, **AI-powered collaboration tools**, and **virtual assistants** that help manage workloads.
- **Learning**: AI-driven platforms like **Duolingo** and **Coursera** are revolutionizing education by providing personalized learning experiences, tracking progress, and recommending courses based on individual preferences.
- **Personal Development**: AI can assist in personal growth by recommending books, courses,

and wellness routines. **AI-powered fitness apps** like **MyFitnessPal** and **Headspace** use AI to guide users in their fitness and mental health journeys.

Address Common Misconceptions and Fears About AI

While AI brings many benefits, it also raises concerns. Some common misconceptions include:

- **AI Will Replace All Jobs**: While AI will automate some tasks, it is more likely to change the nature of work, rather than eliminate jobs. New roles will emerge, and workers will need to adapt by developing new skills.
- **AI Is Unpredictable and Dangerous**: Many people fear AI because of its potential to act in ways that are not easily understood. However, AI development is heavily regulated and monitored to ensure it is safe and ethical. AI models are trained with strict guidelines and oversight.
- **AI Can Think Like Humans**: AI is still far from achieving true human-like intelligence. While AI can perform complex tasks, it cannot truly understand context, emotions, and the nuances of human behavior.

Conclusion

Chapter 2 introduces **AI** as a rapidly advancing field that is already transforming industries and improving everyday life. Understanding the basics of AI, its history, and its potential benefits will lay a solid foundation for readers to explore more complex AI concepts in the chapters to come. By addressing common fears and misconceptions, this chapter aims to demystify AI and highlight its positive impact on society.

Chapter 3

Understanding the Basics of AI

How Does AI Work?

AI works by simulating human intelligence through algorithms and models that can learn from data, make decisions, and solve problems. The process of AI typically involves the following steps:

1. **Input Data**: AI systems begin by receiving data (e.g., text, images, numbers, etc.). This data is the foundation for training the system.

2. **Processing**: The system uses algorithms to analyze the data. These algorithms process the data to find patterns, relationships, or important features.

3. **Learning**: Through **Machine Learning** (ML), AI systems "learn" from the data. This means they can identify patterns or trends without being explicitly programmed for every possible situation.

4. **Decision-Making**: Based on the learned patterns, AI can make decisions or predictions, which could be anything from classifying an image to recommending a

product.

5. **Output:** The AI produces an output, which could be a recommendation, a prediction, or a classification based on the data it processed.

Basic AI Concepts Like Data, Algorithms, and Models

1. **Data**:

Data is the raw information that AI systems use to learn and make decisions. This data can come in various forms, such as images, text, numbers, or even audio. The more high-quality data an AI system has, the better it can "learn" and provide accurate results.

For example, if an AI is being trained to recognize dogs in images, the data would consist of thousands of labeled images of dogs (and non-dogs) for the AI to learn from.

2. **Algorithms**:

An **algorithm** is a set of rules or instructions that guide the AI in processing data, identifying patterns, and making decisions. Algorithms help the AI system understand the relationships in the data and how to use them to predict or classify new data.

For example, an algorithm used in spam detection might analyze email content and learn to classify emails as either **spam** or **not spam** based on certain features like keywords, sender, or formatting.

3. Models:

A **model** is a mathematical representation of the relationships and patterns in the data. After training, the AI system uses the model to make predictions or decisions on new, unseen data. The model is the "trained" version of the algorithm that has learned from the data.

For example, a model trained on images of cats and dogs can be used to classify new images as either a cat or a dog.

Training AI with Data and the Idea of Patterns and Predictions

The process of training an AI system involves feeding it large amounts of data so that it can learn patterns, trends, and relationships in that data. Here's how it works:

1. Training the Model:

AI systems are trained using labeled data (known as **supervised learning**) or unlabeled data (known as **unsupervised learning**). During training, the AI adjusts its internal settings (parameters) to minimize errors in its predictions or classifications. For example, if an AI is classifying images of cats and dogs, it will adjust its model each time it incorrectly classifies an image.

2. Patterns:

AI systems learn to recognize patterns in the data. For instance, if you're training an AI to recognize spam emails, it will learn common patterns in spam emails, like certain words or phrases, the sender's email address, or unusual formatting.

3. **Predictions:**

After training, the AI can make predictions about new, unseen data. For example, once trained, the spam filter AI can predict whether a new email is spam or not based on the patterns it has learned.

The more high-quality data the AI is trained on, the better it becomes at recognizing patterns and making accurate predictions.

Types of AI Systems

AI systems can be categorized based on their capabilities and tasks. There are two primary types of AI systems:

1. **Narrow AI (Weak AI):**

   - **Narrow AI** refers to AI systems that are designed and trained to perform a specific task or a set of related tasks. These systems are highly effective at what they do but are limited to that one task.

     Examples of Narrow AI include **Google Search**, **Siri**, **Netflix** recommendations, and **spam filters**. These systems perform specific functions well but cannot perform tasks outside of their designed purpose.

2. **General AI (Strong AI):**

   - **General AI** refers to a more advanced, theoretical

form of AI that can perform any intellectual task that a human can do. It would have the ability to understand, learn, and apply knowledge across a wide range of activities without being specifically trained for each task.

General AI is still a concept and has not yet been realized. It would be able to think, reason, and make decisions autonomously across various domains, similar to human cognition.

Narrow AI vs. General AI: What Are the Differences, and Why Does It Matter?

- **Narrow AI** is already widespread and powers many of the applications we use daily, such as voice assistants, image recognition, and recommendation systems. Narrow AI is designed to excel at one task and is limited to the data and instructions it was trained on. It's **specialized**, but not capable of performing tasks outside of its designated purpose.

- **General AI**, on the other hand, is a more advanced and flexible system that would be capable of performing any cognitive task a human can do. This type of AI would not be confined to a narrow scope and would have the capacity to adapt to new situations, learn new tasks, and apply knowledge across different domains. **General AI** is still theoretical and has not yet been realized.

The distinction between these types of AI is important because Narrow AI is what we're using today in almost all practical applications, while General AI would require significant advances in both technology and understanding of human cognition. The rise of Narrow AI is what is currently shaping industries and everyday life, while General AI remains a future goal.

Examples of Narrow AI in Daily Life

1. **Siri and Google Assistant**: These AI-powered virtual assistants use **natural language processing** (NLP) to understand voice commands and provide responses or actions (e.g., setting reminders, sending texts, or providing weather updates). They are examples of **Narrow AI** since they specialize in voice recognition and certain tasks but cannot perform tasks outside of their scope.

2. **Netflix Recommendations**: Netflix uses AI to analyze your viewing history and recommend shows and movies based on your preferences. The recommendation system uses **collaborative filtering** and **content-based filtering** algorithms to make personalized suggestions, making it a classic example **of Narrow AI**.

3. **Google Search**: Google's search engine uses AI algorithms to rank and display search results based on

the relevance and quality of the content. It processes millions of web pages to deliver the most relevant results for your query, another example of **Narrow AI**.

4. **Spam Filters**: Email systems use AI to filter out spam by analyzing the content of incoming messages and identifying patterns indicative of spam. This is a task-specific application of **Narrow AI**, designed to classify and filter emails.

Basic Components of AI
Data: Why Data is Crucial for AI Systems

Data is the foundation of AI. AI systems learn from data by identifying patterns and using these patterns to make predictions or decisions. The more high-quality and relevant data an AI has, the better it can perform. For example:

- In healthcare, AI uses data from medical records, images, and patient histories to make diagnoses.
- In e-commerce, AI uses user behavior data to recommend products.

Without data, AI would have no information to learn from or base its decisions on.

Algorithms: How They Help AI Make Decisions

An **algorithm** is a set of instructions that guides the AI in processing data. Algorithms enable AI to recognize patterns, make decisions, and predict outcomes. For example:

- A decision tree algorithm might be used in spam filtering to categorize emails.
- A k-nearest neighbors algorithm might be used in image recognition to classify images based on similarity to other images.

Algorithms are the "brains" behind how AI processes and interprets data.

Training & Testing AI Models: A Beginner-Friendly Explanation

Training an AI model involves providing it with large amounts of labeled data, allowing it to learn from this data and make predictions. For instance:

- **Training**: If you're training an AI to recognize cats in images, you provide it with thousands of labeled images of cats and non-cats. The AI adjusts its model based on this data, learning to identify key features that define a cat.
- **Testing**: Once trained, the AI is tested with new, unseen data to evaluate its performance. If the AI correctly identifies cats in the test images, it means the model is working well.

In the real world, **training** involves refining the model until it can make accurate predictions or decisions, while

testing ensures that the model generalizes well to new data.

Conclusion

Chapter 3 introduces the core concepts of how AI works, from data and algorithms to training models and making predictions. Understanding these basic building blocks is crucial for beginners who want to dive deeper into AI and harness its potential for solving real-world problems. With this foundational knowledge, readers will be prepared to explore more complex AI topics and applications in the following chapters.

Chapter 4

Everyday Applications of AI

AI in Daily Life

AI has become an integral part of everyday life, with applications that make tasks easier, more efficient, and personalized. Below are some common examples of AI used in daily life:

Virtual Assistants (e.g., Siri, Alexa, Google Assistant)

Virtual Assistants use AI to understand and respond to voice commands, helping users perform tasks hands-free. These assistants use **Natural Language Processing (NLP)** to interpret spoken language and **Machine Learning (ML)** to improve their responses over time.
Examples:
- **Siri** (Apple) responds to voice commands on Apple devices and can help with tasks like sending messages, setting reminders, and providing directions.

- **Google Assistant** (Google) integrates with various devices and can control smart home products, answer questions, set appointments, and more.
- **Alexa** (Amazon) is used in **Amazon Echo** devices to control music, smart home devices, and provide information like weather updates and news.

Virtual assistants are powered by AI to make interactions more natural and efficient, improving productivity and convenience.

Personalized Recommendations (e.g., Netflix, YouTube, Spotify)

AI plays a major role in delivering **personalized experiences** across entertainment platforms by recommending content based on user preferences, viewing history, and behavior patterns.

- **Netflix**: Uses collaborative filtering and content-based filtering algorithms to recommend movies and TV shows based on what you've watched, what similar users watch, and even the time of day you watch.
- **YouTube**: AI analyzes your video history to suggest videos that align with your interests, whether for entertainment, education, or music.

- **Spotify**: Uses AI to create personalized playlists like Discover Weekly, recommending music based on your listening habits, artist preferences, and song ratings.

These recommendation systems save time and enhance user experience by helping people discover content they might enjoy without needing to search for it.

Smart Home Devices (e.g., smart thermostats, smart lights)

Smart home devices use AI to automate and optimize household tasks, making homes more energy-efficient, secure, and convenient. AI helps these devices learn from your habits and preferences to improve performance.

- **Smart Thermostats** (e.g., **Nest**): Learn your temperature preferences over time and adjust your home's heating or cooling automatically based on your schedule or environmental conditions, saving energy and money.
- **Smart Lights** (e.g., **Philips Hue**): AI-powered lights can adjust brightness and color based on time of day, or even respond to voice commands or app instructions.
- **Smart Security Cameras**: AI is used in home security cameras (e.g., **Ring**) to detect movement,

recognize faces, and differentiate between people and animals.

These devices simplify daily living by automating tasks, increasing energy efficiency, and improving comfort and security.

AI in Communication: Email Filters, Chatbots, and Translation Tools

AI also enhances communication by making it more efficient and accessible through features like email filtering, chatbots, and real-time translation.

- **Email Filters**: AI-powered spam filters (e.g., **Gmail's** filter) automatically detect and move unwanted emails to the spam folder. They analyze patterns in your emails (such as the sender, subject line, and content) to determine if an email is spam.
- **Chatbots**: Many websites and services use AI-driven chatbots to provide instant customer support. These chatbots can answer frequently asked questions, troubleshoot problems, and guide users through processes, all based on AI algorithms that improve over time.
- **Translation Tools**: AI is used in tools like **Google Translate** to provide real-time translations between languages. AI models can learn the nuances of languages and improve their

accuracy over time.

These AI applications streamline communication, reduce manual effort, and make tasks like customer support and language translation faster and more accessible.

AI for Personal Productivity

AI is a powerful tool for enhancing personal productivity. It helps manage tasks, organize schedules, and assist with writing, allowing individuals to focus on more important and creative activities.

Tools for Organizing Tasks, Emails, and Calendars Using AI

AI-based productivity tools can automate organizational tasks, helping users stay on top of their work and personal schedules.

Task Management: AI-powered tools like **Todoist** or **Trello** can prioritize tasks, set reminders, and even suggest optimal times for completing tasks based on your habits and work patterns.

Email Management: AI tools such as **Google's Smart Compose** or **Clean Email** can help you organize your inbox by automatically categorizing emails, suggesting responses, or unsubscribing from unwanted newsletters.

Calendar Management: AI can assist in scheduling

meetings and appointments. **Google Calendar** uses AI to suggest meeting times that fit your schedule and even analyzes your calendar to find time slots for deep work.

These tools help save time by automating mundane tasks and ensuring that users stay organized and efficient.

AI-Driven Note-Taking and Writing Assistants (e.g., Grammarly, Notion AI)

AI can also assist with writing and note-taking, making the process faster, more accurate, and more professional.

- **Grammarly**: This AI-powered writing assistant checks for grammar, punctuation, style, and tone, offering real-time suggestions to improve the clarity and readability of your writing.
- **Notion AI**: Notion's AI capabilities help with note-taking, brainstorming, and content generation. It can summarize text, suggest ideas, and even help create to-do lists or track goals.
- **Otter.ai**: This app uses AI to transcribe spoken words into text, making it useful for meetings, lectures, or interviews. It can also identify key themes and topics in the conversation.

These AI-driven tools assist in creating polished, professional content and keeping track of important information, enhancing productivity and reducing the time spent on manual tasks.

AI for Health and Wellness

AI is revolutionizing the health and wellness industry by offering personalized recommendations, enhancing fitness tracking, and even providing diagnostic insights.

AI Apps for Fitness Tracking, Mental Health, and Nutrition (e.g., MyFitnessPal, Headspace)

AI-based apps are becoming popular for tracking fitness, improving mental health, and managing nutrition.

- **MyFitnessPal**: This app uses AI to track your daily food intake, exercise routines, and fitness progress. It provides personalized feedback and suggestions based on your goals (e.g., weight loss, muscle gain).
- **Headspace**: A meditation and mindfulness app that uses AI to offer personalized meditation routines based on your mood, stress levels, and goals.
- **Sleep Tracking**: Apps like **Sleep Cycle** use AI to monitor your sleep patterns and provide insights on how to improve sleep quality based on data like sleep stages, disturbances, and overall sleep duration.

These AI apps make it easier to maintain a healthy

lifestyle by offering personalized insights and improving self-awareness in fitness, diet, and mental health.

AI-Powered Health Diagnostics and Personal Health Monitoring

AI is also being used in the medical field to aid in diagnostics, patient care, and personal health monitoring.

- **AI in Diagnostics**: AI algorithms can analyze medical images (e.g., X-rays, MRIs, CT scans) to detect conditions such as tumors, fractures, or heart disease more quickly and accurately than humans. Companies like **Zebra Medical Vision** use AI to interpret medical data and assist doctors in diagnosing diseases.

- **Wearable Health Devices**: Devices like **Apple Watch** and **Fitbit** use AI to monitor heart rate, track activity, and even detect irregularities (such as abnormal heart rhythms). AI-powered apps can alert users to potential health risks and suggest lifestyle changes.

- **Personalized Medicine**: AI is used to analyze a patient's genetic data, medical history, and lifestyle to suggest personalized treatments or medications, optimizing healthcare outcomes.

AI is becoming an indispensable tool in healthcare, offering early detection, personalized treatment plans, and ongoing health monitoring, leading to better health outcomes.

Conclusion

In Chapter 4, we explored how AI is seamlessly integrated into everyday life, from virtual assistants and personalized recommendations to smart home devices and productivity tools. AI is enhancing daily tasks, improving efficiency, and providing personalized experiences. Additionally, in the fields of health and wellness, AI is helping individuals track their fitness, manage their mental health, and even assist in medical diagnostics. These applications demonstrate how AI is not just a futuristic concept, but a present-day tool that is making life easier, healthier, and more productive.

With these insights, readers can begin to see the practical benefits of incorporating AI into their own daily routines and workflows.

Chapter 5

Using AI Tools and Platforms

Intro to Popular AI Tools

In this section, we will introduce some of the most popular AI tools that you can use for various purposes, such as content creation, image generation, and learning enhancement.

AI Writing Assistants

AI writing assistants are tools that leverage **Natural Language Processing (NLP)** to help users generate, refine, and optimize written content. These tools are especially useful for content creators, marketers, and businesses that need to produce high-quality written material efficiently.

ChatGPT (by OpenAI):

- **ChatGPT** is a conversational AI model developed by OpenAI, capable of generating human-like text based on prompts. It can help you with a wide range of writing tasks, including generating blog posts, answering questions, drafting emails, and even creating scripts for videos.

- **How it works**: You simply provide a prompt (e.g., "Write a blog post on the benefits of AI in education"), and ChatGPT generates a well-structured response. It can also assist with editing, brainstorming ideas, and summarizing text.

- **Example**: You can use ChatGPT to create an article about a specific topic by prompting it with a few sentences, and it will generate a draft that you can refine and edit.

Copy.ai:
- **Copy.ai** is another AI-powered writing tool designed specifically for marketers and entrepreneurs. It specializes in creating marketing copy, including product descriptions, ad copy, and social media content. Its algorithms are trained on a wide variety of content types, allowing it to generate persuasive and engaging copy.
- **How it works**: You can input a product description or a topic, and Copy.ai will generate several variations of headlines, ads, or descriptions. It's ideal for anyone who needs to create compelling content quickly.
- **Example**: A marketer could use Copy.ai to generate multiple variations of an ad campaign for

a new product, then choose the one that resonates best with their target audience.

Writesonic:

- **Writesonic** is a versatile writing tool that can generate blog posts, landing pages, social media posts, and more. It leverages AI to generate SEO-friendly content, making it an excellent choice for content marketers and bloggers looking to improve their online presence.
- **How it works**: You provide a topic or title, and Writesonic generates well-structured articles or web pages that are optimized for search engines.
- **Example**: If you need a blog post on a specific subject, you can use Writesonic to quickly generate an SEO-optimized article that you can refine and publish.

These AI tools significantly speed up the content creation process, allowing writers and marketers to produce high-quality material with minimal effort.

AI Image Creation

AI image creation platforms allow users to generate custom artwork and images from text descriptions. These tools are powered by deep learning models, such as **Generative Adversarial Networks (GANs)**, to generate unique and creative visual content.

MidJourney:
- **MidJourney** is an AI-powered image generation platform known for creating stunning, artistic images from text prompts. It is especially popular with digital artists, designers, and creatives who need unique images for projects.
- **How it works**: Users input a description of the image they want (e.g., "A futuristic city at sunset"), and MidJourney generates a variety of artistic interpretations of that prompt.
- **Example**: You could use MidJourney to create concept art for a video game or generate an image for a book cover based on a specific theme.

DALL-E (by OpenAI):
- **DALL-E** is an AI system that generates images from textual descriptions. It is capable of creating highly detailed and imaginative images by combining multiple elements into a cohesive scene.
- **How it works**: By providing a text prompt (e.g., "A two-story house made of chocolate"), DALL-E can create an original image that matches the description.
- **Example**: A graphic designer can use DALL-E to

quickly generate unique visual concepts for advertising or branding campaigns.

DeepArt:

- **DeepArt** uses AI to transform photos into artwork in the style of famous artists, like Van Gogh or Picasso. It applies deep neural networks to create stunning artistic effects based on the original photo.
- **How it works**: You upload an image, select an artistic style, and DeepArt applies that style to your photo, resulting in a unique piece of art.
- **Example**: You can use DeepArt to turn personal photos into artistic representations, perfect for social media content or personalized gifts.

These AI-powered image creation tools are perfect for anyone looking to generate custom images, whether for personal projects, marketing, or creative endeavors.

AI-Powered Learning Platforms

AI is transforming the way we learn by providing personalized and adaptive learning experiences. AI-powered learning platforms can enhance educational experiences, optimize lesson plans, and help learners improve their skills more efficiently.

Duolingo:

- **Duolingo** is a popular language-learning app that uses AI to create personalized lessons for learners. The app adapts to your progress, providing practice exercises tailored to your strengths and weaknesses.
- **How it works**: Duolingo uses AI to adjust the difficulty of lessons, review words or phrases you struggle with, and suggest new vocabulary based on your learning pattern.
- **Example:** If you're learning Spanish, Duolingo will adjust the content based on how well you perform in previous lessons, ensuring that you are always challenged at the right level.

Coursera:

- **Coursera** is an online learning platform that partners with top universities to offer courses in various subjects. AI plays a key role in recommending courses based on your interests, skills, and learning history.
- **How it works**: Coursera uses AI to recommend personalized learning paths based on your goals, helping you find relevant courses. It also provides adaptive learning features to help you progress through lessons at your own pace.
- **Example**: If you've completed a course on data

science, Coursera might suggest advanced machine learning or AI courses as the next step in your learning journey.

These AI-powered platforms make learning more personalized, engaging, and efficient by adapting to your needs and helping you stay on track.

Getting Started with AI Tools

Getting started with AI tools doesn't have to be complicated. Here's how beginners can sign up for AI platforms and begin using their basic features.

How to Sign Up for AI Platforms and Use Basic Features

1. Sign Up:
- Most AI platforms require you to create an account, which typically involves entering your email address and creating a password. Some platforms also offer **free trials** or **freemium models**, where basic features are free and advanced features require a paid plan.
- **Example**: To use **ChatGPT**, sign up for an OpenAI account. Once signed in, you can start typing prompts in the chat interface.

2. Explore Basic Features:

- Once you've signed up, explore the basic features of the tool. AI platforms usually have tutorials or onboarding processes to guide you through their key functionalities. Start by experimenting with simple tasks to get comfortable.
- **Example**: In **Writesonic**, start by generating a short blog post. Enter a topic or brief description, and let the AI generate content for you. Review and make adjustments as needed.

3. **Set Preferences**:
- Many AI platforms allow you to customize settings to better suit your needs. For example, in **Duolingo**, you can set your learning goals and preferred language.
- **Example:** If you're using **MidJourney**, you can experiment with different styles by modifying your text prompt to suit your artistic preferences.

Step-by-Step Guides on Using AI Tools for Beginners
- **Writing a Blog Post Using AI (ChatGPT):**
  1. Log in to **ChatGPT**.
  2. Type a prompt like "Write a 600-word blog post on the benefits of meditation."
  3. Review the content and refine it to add your personal touch or correct any inaccuracies.

4. Once satisfied, copy the content to your blog platform and publish it.

- **Creating Art Using AI (DALL-E or MidJourney):**
  1. Sign up for MidJourney or DALL-E.
  2. Enter a text prompt describing the image you want to generate (e.g., "A surreal landscape with flying fish").
  3. Choose your preferred version from the generated options and download the image.

- **Automating Tasks Using AI (Zapier):**
  1. Sign up for **Zapier** and link your apps (e.g., Gmail and Google Sheets).
  2. Create a "Zap" to automate a task, like automatically saving email attachments to a specific Google Drive folder.
  3. Set triggers (e.g., "When I receive an email with an attachment") and actions (e.g., "Save the attachment to Google Drive").

Practical Examples and Exercises

To help readers get hands-on experience with AI, here are some simple exercises they can try:

1. Creating an AI-Generated Image (MidJourney or DALL-E)

- **Exercise**: Have readers sign up for MidJourney or DALL-E and experiment with creating an image from a text prompt. For example, prompt the tool to create an image of "a futuristic city at night with flying cars" and explore the different variations and styles.

2. Writing an Article Using AI (ChatGPT or Writesonic)

- **Exercise**: Ask readers to write a 500-word article on a topic of their choice using ChatGPT or Writesonic. They should review the AI-generated content, add their own insights, and refine it to suit their voice and style.

3. Using AI to Analyze Personal Data (Google Analytics, Fitbit)

- **Exercise**: If readers use **Google Analytics** or **Fitbit**, ask them to explore the AI-driven insights provided by these platforms. For example, analyze data on website traffic or track fitness progress using AI-powered recommendations.

Conclusion

Chapter 5 has introduced some of the most popular AI tools available today, including **AI writing assistants**, **image creation platforms**, and **AI-powered learning tools**. With the step-by-step guides and practical exercises provided, readers can begin using these tools to enhance their productivity, creativity, and learning. Whether it's writing blog posts, creating unique artwork, or automating tasks, AI tools empower users to accomplish more with less effort. By following the exercises in this chapter, readers will gain valuable hands-on experience and start integrating AI into their daily routines.

Chapter 6

AI for Personal Finance and Productivity

Artificial Intelligence (AI) is not only transforming industries like healthcare, marketing, and entertainment, but it is also revolutionizing how we manage our personal finances, stay productive, and grow our careers. In this chapter, we will explore how AI can be applied in these areas, helping you save time, make smarter financial decisions, and optimize your work life. Whether you're looking for tools to help with budgeting, saving, investing, managing your time, or advancing your career, AI can provide powerful solutions.

AI in Financial Management

AI has become an indispensable tool in personal finance, offering smart solutions for budgeting, saving, investing, and financial planning. With the help of AI, individuals can make more informed decisions, stay on top of their finances, and optimize their economic growth. Below are some AI-driven tools and platforms changing how we manage our money.

Personal Finance Apps that Use AI for Budgeting, Saving, and Investing

AI-powered personal finance apps can automate many aspects of financial management. These apps analyze your spending patterns, help you set goals, and offer actionable insights to save more and invest smarter.

Mint:

- **Mint** is one of the most popular AI-powered budgeting apps. It automatically syncs with your bank accounts, credit cards, and bills to track your spending and categorize expenses. Mint uses AI to analyze your financial habits, identify areas where you can save, and offer personalized budgeting advice.

- How it works: Mint's AI algorithms classify your transactions and create a budget based on your income and spending habits. It can even send alerts if you're nearing your budget limit or if a bill is due soon. Over time, Mint learns about your spending patterns and adapts its suggestions to optimize your budget.

- **Example**: You might receive a notification from Mint saying, "You spent 20% more on dining out this month than last month. Try reducing your restaurant spending to save more."

Acorns:

- **Acorns** is a micro-investing app that automatically invests spare change from everyday purchases into diversified portfolios. It uses AI to personalize investment strategies based on your financial goals and risk tolerance.
- **How it works**: Acorns rounds up your purchases to the nearest dollar and invests the spare change. For example, if you buy a coffee for 3.50, Acorns will round up to4.00 and invest the $0.50 difference. The AI behind Acorns tailors your investment portfolio based on your preferences, adjusting your risk levels and asset allocation over time.
- **Example**: Acorns might suggest reallocating your investments into more aggressive stocks if you're a young investor with a long time horizon or move toward more conservative bonds as you approach retirement.

Other Finance Apps:

Apps like **YNAB (You Need A Budget)** and **Personal Capital** use AI to track spending, optimize savings, and provide investment insights. These apps offer personalized financial planning, tax-saving strategies, and real-time budgeting adjustments, making it easier to meet your financial goals.

AI in these apps makes financial management simpler, more personalized, and more efficient, empowering you to take control of your money with minimal effort.

AI-Driven Stock Analysis Tools and Financial Planning

AI is also transforming the way we analyze stocks and plan our financial future. By utilizing vast amounts of data, AI tools can offer real-time insights into market trends, stock performance, and personalized investment strategies.

Stock Analysis Tools (e.g., Trade Ideas, Zacks, Alpha Vantage):

- **Trade Ideas** uses AI to scan the stock market for trading opportunities, offering real-time alerts about stocks that meet certain criteria. The platform's AI algorithms analyze market data, news, and trends to provide stock recommendations and trading strategies.
- **Zacks** uses AI to provide stock ratings and financial insights. It analyzes financial reports, earnings calls, and other relevant data to evaluate stock performance and predict future movements.
- **Alpha Vantage** offers API services for stock analysis, using machine learning models to predict

stock prices and provide real-time market updates.

These tools are incredibly useful for investors who want to make data-driven decisions without spending hours manually analyzing the market.

AI in Financial Planning (e.g., Betterment, Wealthfront):

- **Betterment** and **Wealthfront** are **robo-advisors** that use AI to create personalized investment portfolios. These platforms take your financial goals, risk tolerance, and time horizon and use AI algorithms to build and manage an investment portfolio that is tailored specifically to you.
- **How it works**: After answering a few questions about your financial situation and goals, the AI behind these platforms generates a diversified portfolio of stocks and bonds, automatically rebalancing it over time as market conditions change.
- **Example**: If your risk profile changes (for example, if you move from a high-risk to a low-risk investor), these platforms will adjust your portfolio to meet your new preferences.

AI-driven financial planning tools help individuals make

smarter investment decisions, and retirement plan, and optimize their financial portfolios with little to no manual effort.

Boosting Personal Productivity with AI

AI doesn't just help with finance; it's also a game-changer for personal productivity. Whether you need help managing your time, staying focused, or automating repetitive tasks, AI tools can make your work life more efficient and organized.

AI Tools for Time Management, Focus, and Goal-Setting

Effective time management and goal-setting are crucial for productivity, and AI can help streamline these processes.

RescueTime:
- **RescueTime** is an AI-powered tool that tracks how you spend your time on your computer or mobile devices. It helps you identify time-wasting habits, set productivity goals, and improve focus.
- **How it works**: RescueTime runs in the background and categorizes your activities (e.g., time spent on social media, writing emails, or working on projects). It then generates reports to help you understand your productivity patterns

and make adjustments.
- **Example**: If RescueTime detects that you're spending too much time on non-productive activities, it can send reminders or suggest time blocks for focused work.

Trello:
- **Trello** is a project management tool that uses AI to help you organize tasks and track progress. It allows you to create boards, assign tasks, set deadlines, and collaborate with teams. Trello uses AI to automate certain tasks and set reminders for upcoming deadlines.
- **How it works**: You can create a Trello board for a project, and the AI will help you prioritize tasks, set deadlines, and send reminders when tasks are due. It also integrates with other productivity tools, such as Slack and Google Calendar.
- **Example**: Trello might automatically categorize tasks based on urgency and complexity, ensuring that you focus on high-priority items first.

Todoist:
- **Todoist** is a task management app that uses AI to help you organize your daily tasks and goals. It can help you prioritize tasks based on deadlines, importance, and your work habits.

- **How it works**: Todoist analyzes your productivity patterns to suggest the best times to complete tasks. It also helps you break down large projects into smaller, more manageable tasks.
- **Example**: Todoist can suggest the optimal time for a task based on your previous activities and productivity patterns, ensuring that you're working at your most efficient times.

These AI tools for time management and goal-setting help you stay organized, focused, and productive, allowing you to get more done in less time.

Automating Repetitive Tasks with AI
One of the biggest advantages of AI is its ability to automate repetitive tasks, freeing up more time for creative and high-value work. AI automation tools can connect different apps, perform routine tasks, and streamline workflows.

Zapier:
- **Zapier** is an automation tool that connects over 2,000 apps, enabling you to automate tasks without writing code. You can create "Zaps" that automatically trigger actions across multiple apps based on specific events.
- **How it works**: For example, you can create a Zap

to automatically save email attachments from Gmail to Google Drive or create a task in Trello whenever a new email is received.

- **Example**: You can use Zapier to automate your social media posts, ensuring that content is published at the optimal times without any manual intervention.

IFTTT (If This Then That):

- **IFTTT** is another automation tool that connects different apps and services to perform tasks automatically. It allows you to create conditional statements (e.g., "If I receive an email with an attachment, then save it to Dropbox").
- **How it works**: IFTTT creates a seamless connection between apps like Instagram, Google Sheets, and Slack, automating tasks like posting images, organizing files, or sending alerts.
- **Example**: You can create an IFTTT applet to automatically back up photos from your Instagram account to Google Photos or send a daily summary of your calendar events to Slack.

By automating routine tasks, you can focus more on high-value work and creative endeavors, increasing your productivity in the process.

AI in Career Development

AI is not just transforming personal finance and productivity—it's also reshaping the job market and creating new career opportunities. Whether you're looking for a new job, improving your skills, or building a resume, AI tools can give you a competitive edge.

How AI Is Reshaping Job Markets and Creating New Career Opportunities

AI is automating many routine jobs, but it is also creating new career opportunities in fields like AI development, data science, machine learning, and robotics. As AI continues to evolve, new roles and industries will emerge that require specialized knowledge and skills.

Automation of Routine Jobs: AI is automating tasks in areas such as customer service, data entry, and manufacturing. While some jobs are being replaced, new roles are being created in fields related to AI and technology.

New Career Opportunities: Roles like **AI ethics consultant**, **data scientist**, and **robotics engineer** are becoming increasingly important. Professionals with expertise in AI technologies are in high demand, and the job market is evolving to accommodate these needs.

Using AI Tools for Resume Building, Job Search, and Skill Development

AI can also assist you in your job search and career development by providing personalized recommendations, helping you optimize your resume, and suggesting skill development opportunities.

Resume Building (e.g., Rezi, Jobscan):
- **Rezi** and **Jobscan** use AI to optimize your resume for specific job descriptions. These tools analyze the job posting and suggest ways to tailor your resume to match the employer's requirements, ensuring that you pass through Applicant Tracking Systems (ATS).
- **Example**: Jobscan compares your resume to a job description and provides suggestions on how to improve your resume by adding relevant keywords and skills.

Job Search (e.g., LinkedIn, ZipRecruiter):
- **LinkedIn** and **ZipRecruiter** use AI to recommend job opportunities based on your profile, skills, and career goals. These platforms analyze your resume, past job searches, and interactions to provide personalized job recommendations.

- **Example**: If you've been applying for marketing positions, LinkedIn might suggest similar roles in marketing or sales that match your skills.

Skill Development (e.g., Coursera, Udemy, LinkedIn Learning):

- AI-powered learning platforms like **Coursera**, **Udemy**, and **LinkedIn** Learning offer personalized course recommendations based on your career goals and current skills. These platforms use AI to suggest the best courses for you to develop new skills and enhance your career prospects.
- **Example**: If you're interested in data science, Coursera might recommend courses on machine learning, Python, and data visualization based on your previous learning history.

Conclusion

AI is reshaping how we manage our finances, boost our productivity, and develop our careers. From personal finance apps that help us budget and invest smarter to productivity tools that automate tasks and manage time effectively, AI is becoming an essential tool for achieving our goals. By leveraging AI in these areas, individuals can save time, make smarter decisions, and stay ahead in an ever-changing job market. Whether you're optimizing your financial strategies, improving productivity, or advancing your career, AI offers powerful tools that can help you succeed.

Chapter 7

Understanding AI Ethics and Privacy

As artificial intelligence (AI) continues to evolve and integrate into various aspects of our daily lives, understanding its ethical implications and the associated privacy concerns is crucial. While AI offers immense potential to improve efficiency, create new opportunities, and solve complex problems, it also presents challenges related to fairness, bias, accountability, and the protection of personal information. This chapter explores the ethical considerations of AI, addresses privacy concerns, and examines the future of AI and its impact on society.

Ethical Considerations of AI

AI technologies are reshaping industries and transforming the way we interact with the world. However, as AI systems become more autonomous and integrated into decision-making processes, it is essential to address the ethical challenges they pose. Ethical AI development ensures that AI systems are created and used in ways that align with societal values and promote fairness, transparency, and accountability.

The Role of Bias in AI and How It Affects Decision-Making

One of the most significant ethical concerns in AI is **bias**. Bias can be introduced into AI systems in various ways—through the data used to train models, the design of the algorithms, and the way AI is deployed. If AI systems are biased, they can perpetuate discrimination and inequality, especially in critical areas such as hiring, law enforcement, and healthcare.

- **Bias in Hiring Algorithms:**
  Many companies use AI-driven tools to help with recruitment and hiring. These algorithms often screen resumes, assess candidate qualifications, and even conduct interviews. However, if the training data used to develop these systems is biased (e.g., historical data reflecting gender or racial discrimination), the AI may favor certain groups over others.
  Example: In some cases, hiring algorithms have been found to favor male candidates for technical roles because the historical data used to train the AI reflected a male-dominated workforce. This can result in unintentional discrimination against

women or other underrepresented groups.

- **Bias in Facial Recognition:**
  Facial recognition technology, powered by AI, is increasingly used for security, identification, and surveillance. However, studies have shown that facial recognition systems are less accurate at identifying people with darker skin tones and women. This bias in the technology can lead to misidentifications, wrongful arrests, and privacy violations.
  Example: In a well-known case, facial recognition software used by law enforcement agencies struggled to accurately identify Black faces, leading to concerns about racial profiling and wrongful arrests.

- **Addressing Bias:**
  To mitigate bias, AI developers need to ensure that their algorithms are trained on diverse and representative datasets. **Bias audits**—systematic assessments of AI systems to identify and address bias—are essential. Additionally, AI systems should be regularly updated to reflect societal changes and ensure fairness in decision-making.

How AI Can Be Used Responsibly and Ethically

AI systems should be developed and used in ways that align with ethical principles, ensuring that they are transparent, accountable, and beneficial to society. Ethical AI development involves creating systems that prioritize human welfare and respect fundamental rights.

- **Transparency and Accountability**: AI systems must be transparent, meaning that users and stakeholders can understand how the system works and how decisions are made. This is especially important when AI is used in critical areas like healthcare, finance, and law enforcement. AI developers should also be held accountable for the actions of their systems, ensuring that there is a clear process for addressing any harm caused by AI decisions.

- **Fairness and Inclusivity**: Ethical AI development should prioritize fairness by ensuring that AI systems do not discriminate against any group. Developers should actively seek to design systems that are inclusive, promoting equality and diversity in their outcomes.

- **Ethical Guidelines and Regulations**: Governments, organizations, and researchers must work together to establish ethical guidelines and regulations for AI development and deployment. This includes creating frameworks for ethical AI use in different industries, ensuring that AI benefits society while minimizing harm.

Privacy Concerns with AI

As AI becomes more integrated into our daily lives, privacy concerns are increasingly at the forefront. AI systems often rely on vast amounts of data, much of which is personal and sensitive. The way AI collects, processes, and uses this data can have serious implications for individual privacy and data security.

How AI Systems Collect and Use Personal Data

AI systems typically require large datasets to function effectively, and much of this data comes from users. The collection and use of personal data raise important questions about consent, transparency, and security.

- **Data Collection**:
  AI systems collect personal data from various sources, such as social media, smart devices, health apps, and online transactions. For example, voice assistants like **Amazon Alexa** and **Google Assistant** collect voice data to improve their responses and functionality. Similarly, apps like **Fitbit** and **MyFitnessPal** collect health data to

provide personalized recommendations.

- **Data Usage**:
  Once collected, the data is used to train AI algorithms, improve system performance, and generate personalized recommendations. For example, AI-powered recommendation engines on platforms like Netflix and Spotify use your viewing or listening history to suggest new movies, shows, or music. In healthcare, AI can analyze medical records to assist with diagnoses and treatment plans.

- **Privacy Risks**:
  The collection of personal data by AI systems presents significant privacy risks. Without proper safeguards, this data could be accessed by unauthorized parties, leading to data breaches or misuse. Additionally, AI systems may track users' activities without their knowledge or consent, violating personal privacy.

Tips on Protecting Your Privacy When Using AI Tools

To minimize privacy risks when using AI tools, individuals should take proactive steps to protect their personal data and ensure that AI systems are used responsibly.

- **Review Privacy Policies**: Always read the privacy policies of the AI tools you use. Ensure that you understand how your data will be collected, stored, and used. Look for tools that are transparent about their data practices and that offer clear explanations about how your information is handled.
- **Limit Data Sharing**: Many AI tools allow you to control the amount of data you share. For example, you can disable certain features in voice assistants (like voice recording) or limit the access that apps have to your data (e.g., location, contacts, etc.). Be mindful of the data you provide and limit sharing when possible.
- **Use Privacy-Preserving Tools**: Some AI tools prioritize privacy and security. For example, **DuckDuckGo** is a search engine that doesn't track your searches, and **ProtonMail** is an encrypted email service that protects your communication from third-party surveillance. Look for privacy-conscious alternatives when using AI-powered tools.
- **Enable Two-Factor Authentication**: For AI tools that store sensitive data, enable two-factor authentication (2FA) to add an extra layer of security. This will help protect your accounts from

unauthorized access, even if your password is compromised.

- **Use Encryption**: When using AI tools for sensitive tasks (e.g., financial apps, health trackers), ensure that the data is encrypted. This ensures that even if the data is intercepted, it cannot be read by unauthorized parties.

By taking these steps, you can better protect your privacy while still benefiting from the advantages AI offers.

The Future of AI and Society

As AI continues to evolve, it will have profound effects on various aspects of society. From automating jobs to transforming industries, the future of AI holds both opportunities and challenges. It is crucial to approach AI development and deployment with a responsible mindset to ensure that it benefits humanity as a whole.

How AI Will Continue to Evolve and Impact Our Lives in the Next Decade

In the coming decade, AI is expected to evolve in several key areas, significantly impacting our lives:

- **Automation and Job Displacement**: AI will continue to automate routine and manual tasks in industries like manufacturing, transportation, and customer service. While this will lead to increased efficiency, it may also result in job displacement for certain workers. However, AI will also create new job opportunities in fields like AI development, data science, and robotics.

- **Healthcare Advancements**: AI will revolutionize healthcare by improving diagnostics, personalizing treatment plans, and enhancing drug discovery. AI-powered systems will assist doctors in identifying diseases at earlier stages and predicting potential health risks.

- **Smart Cities and Infrastructure**: AI will play a significant role in creating smarter cities, improving traffic management, energy efficiency, and public safety. AI-powered systems will optimize urban planning, enhance transportation networks, and reduce environmental impact.

- **Ethical and Regulatory Challenges**: As AI becomes more integrated into society, it will raise important ethical and regulatory challenges. Governments and organizations will need to develop policies that ensure AI is used responsibly, safely, and fairly.

The Importance of Responsible AI Development and Use

To harness the potential of AI while mitigating its risks, responsible AI development is essential. This involves creating AI systems that are ethical, transparent, and accountable, and ensuring that they are used in ways that benefit society.

Inclusive and Transparent Development: AI developers must ensure that AI systems are inclusive, fair, and transparent. They should actively involve diverse stakeholders in the development process to ensure that AI benefits everyone.

Ethical Governance: Governments, organizations, and institutions must establish ethical frameworks and regulations to guide AI development. These frameworks should prioritize human rights, fairness, privacy, and accountability.

Continuous Monitoring and Adaptation: As AI evolves, it is essential to continuously monitor its impact on society and make necessary adjustments. This includes addressing emerging issues such as AI's impact on jobs, privacy, and social equality.

Conclusion

Chapter 7 examined the crucial link between AI ethics and privacy. While AI offers great potential, its development raises ethical and privacy concerns. Key issues include: bias in AI (especially in hiring and facial recognition, requiring diverse data and audits), the need for responsible AI development (emphasizing transparency, accountability, fairness, and regulation), privacy risks due to AI's reliance on personal data (requiring user vigilance and security measures), and the future impact of AI on various sectors (demanding ongoing ethical consideration and responsible development). Ultimately, realizing AI's potential while minimizing risks requires responsible development, ethical governance, and continuous monitoring to ensure AI benefits humanity equitably.

Chapter 8

AI for Creativity

In the past, creativity was often viewed as a uniquely human trait—something that machines could never replicate. However, with the advent of AI, the boundaries of creativity are expanding. AI is not just a tool for automation or data processing; it is increasingly becoming a collaborator in the creative process. Artists, musicians, writers, and content creators are using AI to enhance their creativity, generate new ideas, and even produce entire works of art.

In this chapter, we will explore how AI is transforming creative fields, the tools that are making this possible, and how AI can serve as a partner in the creative process rather than a mere replacement for human creativity.

AI in Art, Music, and Writing

AI has made significant strides in various creative fields, allowing creators to experiment with new techniques, explore uncharted territories, and produce innovative works that would have been difficult or impossible to create without AI. Let's take a look at how AI is being used in three major creative domains: art, music, and writing.

How AI is Transforming Creative Fields

- **AI-Generated Artwork**: AI is revolutionizing the world of visual art, offering artists new ways to create, explore, and express their ideas. AI algorithms can generate stunning artwork based on user inputs, learn from thousands of existing art styles, and even create original pieces that mimic famous artists like Van Gogh, Picasso, or Rembrandt.

  Example: Tools like **DALL-E** and **DeepArt** have enabled artists to generate new visual concepts by simply describing them in words. DALL-E, an AI model developed by OpenAI, can generate high-quality images from textual descriptions, allowing anyone to create unique artwork by just typing a prompt.

  DALL-E Example: A user might input "a futuristic cityscape with flying cars and neon lights," and DALL-E would generate a completely original image based on that description.

- **DeepArt**: This platform uses AI to transform photographs into artwork in the style of famous artists. By training on thousands of classic works of art, it can take an ordinary photo and apply the visual style of Van Gogh, Monet, or even abstract art styles, creating unique interpretations of the original image.

- **AI in Music Composition**:
  AI is also transforming the music industry. AI-driven tools can generate original compositions in various genres, from classical to electronic music. These tools use machine learning to analyze existing music, identify patterns, and create new melodies, harmonies, and rhythms that are pleasing to the human ear.
  Example: **Aiva** (Artificial Intelligence Virtual Artist) is an AI music composition software that creates original symphonic music. Aiva analyzes thousands of classical music pieces and uses this knowledge to compose original works that sound like they were written by a human composer.
  Aiva Example: Aiva has been used to compose music for films, video games, and commercials, showcasing how AI can create music that evokes emotion and sets the tone for visual media.

- **AI in Writing**:
  In the realm of writing, AI is being used to assist

with generating ideas, drafting content, and even writing entire articles, stories, or poems. AI models like **GPT-3** (the model behind ChatGPT) are capable of producing coherent and contextually relevant text based on prompts provided by the user.

Example: Writers and journalists are using AI to generate article drafts, brainstorm creative ideas, or even assist with writing dialogue for stories. AI writing assistants can help with everything from short blog posts to full-length novels, helping writers overcome writer's block and generate content at a faster pace.

GPT-3 Example: A writer might use GPT-3 to generate a short story based on a theme like "love in the future," and the AI would provide a detailed and creative narrative.

AI for Content Creation

AI has also become a valuable tool for content creators, including marketers, bloggers, social media influencers, and business owners. AI can help streamline the content creation process by assisting with idea generation, writing, and even content optimization.

Using AI to Brainstorm Ideas, Write Articles, or Generate Social Media Content

AI can serve as an invaluable tool for brainstorming new content ideas, writing drafts, and generating social media posts. By analyzing trends, popular topics, and user preferences, AI can help content creators stay relevant and creative.

- **AI for Idea Generation:**
  AI tools can analyze large amounts of data to identify trending topics, emerging keywords, and relevant content ideas. By using AI to track audience interests and preferences, content creators can stay ahead of the curve and produce timely, engaging content.
  Example: **BuzzSumo** is a tool that uses AI to analyze the most shared content on social media, helping content creators identify popular topics and generate fresh ideas for blog posts, videos, and social media content.

- **AI for Writing Articles:**
  AI-powered writing assistants like **Copy.ai**, **Writesonic**, and **Jarvis** (formerly known as Conversion.ai) can help writers draft articles, create marketing copy, and generate website content. These tools use GPT-3 to write coherent and contextually relevant text based on a few input keywords or topics.

Example: A blogger could use Copy.ai to quickly generate an article draft on a topic like "The Benefits of Meditation for Mental Health." The AI would produce a well-structured article that could then be edited and refined by the writer.

- **AI for Social Media Content:**
  AI can assist with creating social media posts by generating text, suggesting hashtags, and even designing visual content. AI tools like Canva use machine learning to recommend design layouts, colors, and fonts based on the content, making it easier for creators to generate engaging posts for Instagram, Facebook, or Twitter.
  Example: A brand manager could use **Lately AI** to analyze past social media posts and determine which types of content perform best with their audience. The AI would then generate new post ideas that align with past successful content.

How AI Can Assist in Enhancing Creativity, Rather Than Replacing It

One common concern about AI in creative fields is that it may replace human artists, writers, and musicians. However, AI is not meant to replace creativity but to enhance it. AI tools can serve as valuable assistants in the creative process, helping creators generate new ideas, overcome creative blocks, and experiment with new styles or techniques.

- **AI as a Creative Assistant:**
  Rather than replacing human creativity, AI can amplify it by providing new perspectives, suggesting novel ideas, and helping creators explore uncharted territory. For example, AI can help a painter create unique digital art styles, assist a musician in composing experimental melodies, or enable a writer to draft ideas quickly.
  Example: A painter might use **DeepArt** to generate digital art in a new style, which could inspire them to create their own original work based on the AI-generated output. Similarly, a writer might use AI-generated poetry as a starting point, refining it with their own creative voice to produce a unique piece.

- **AI as a Tool for Inspiration:**
  AI can also provide inspiration by offering creative suggestions based on input. For instance, a musician could input a few chord progressions into an AI-powered tool like **Amper Music** and receive a variety of music compositions to choose from. These compositions can serve as the foundation for new creative works, which the

musician can then modify and expand upon.

Example: A filmmaker could use AI-generated visual concepts to inspire their set designs or storylines, integrating the AI's suggestions into their artistic vision.

Collaborating with AI

AI should not be viewed as a replacement for human creativity, but rather as a collaborator in the creative process. The most successful artists, writers, and musicians are those who see AI as a creative partner that can help them push the boundaries of their work.

Viewing AI as a Creative Partner, Not Just a Tool

Creativity is a deeply personal and human experience, and AI can be a valuable partner in that process. By leveraging AI tools to explore new ideas, test different approaches, and generate creative outputs, humans can enhance their creative capacity and break through traditional limitations.

- **AI as a Partner in Exploration:**
  AI allows creators to explore ideas they might not have thought of on their own. Whether it's generating new visual compositions, creating novel soundscapes, or suggesting alternative storylines, AI can push creators to think outside the box.

- **Real-Life Examples of Artists, Writers, and Musicians Using AI in Their Creative Process:**
  Artists: The artist **Refik Anadol** uses AI and machine learning to create large-scale installations and digital artworks. By inputting vast amounts of data into AI systems, Anadol generates mesmerizing visuals that explore the intersection of technology and art.

- **Writers**: The science fiction author **Robin Sloan** has used AI to assist in his creative writing process, using AI to generate dialogue, plot ideas, and even character names for his novels.

- **Musicians**: The Grammy-winning composer **Taryn Southern** has collaborated with AI tools like **Amper Music** to compose original music. Southern uses AI-generated compositions as a starting point, incorporating her own artistic direction and voice into the final product.

Conclusion

AI is transforming the creative landscape by providing artists, writers, and musicians with new tools to enhance their work. Rather than replacing creativity, AI serves as a powerful collaborator, helping creators generate ideas, explore new possibilities, and experiment with innovative techniques. Whether you're an artist creating digital paintings, a musician composing symphonic pieces, or a writer drafting stories, AI can amplify your creativity and offer fresh perspectives. By viewing AI as a creative partner, rather than a mere tool, you can unlock new realms of artistic expression and push the boundaries of what's possible in the creative world.

Chapter 9

The Future of AI and What to Expect

Artificial Intelligence (AI) has already begun transforming industries, businesses, and daily life in profound ways. But as AI technology evolves, its impact on the world will only grow, opening new frontiers in innovation, ethics, and societal change. In this chapter, we'll explore the exciting **emerging AI trends**, how AI is poised to address **global challenges**, and the steps we can take to **prepare for the AI-driven future**.

Emerging AI Trends

The future of AI is full of promise and uncertainty. As AI technologies continue to advance, we can expect to see new capabilities, applications, and challenges emerge. Here are some of the most significant trends in AI that are shaping its future.

Artificial General Intelligence (AGI): What Is It, and When Might It Happen?

What Is AGI?

Artificial General Intelligence (AGI) refers to AI systems that possess the ability to understand, learn, and apply knowledge across a wide range of tasks—much like a human being. Unlike **Narrow AI** (which is designed for specific tasks, such as playing chess or recognizing faces), AGI would be able to perform any cognitive task that a human can. AGI would exhibit general intelligence, adaptability, and the capacity for abstract reasoning, creativity, and problem-solving in a wide range of domains.

When Might AGI Happen?

While Narrow AI has made remarkable progress, AGI is still largely theoretical. Experts have varying opinions on when AGI might become a reality. Some believe that AGI could be developed within the next few decades, while others argue that it is still far off, with fundamental scientific and technological breakthroughs needed. The timeline for AGI is highly speculative, and predictions range from 20 to 50 years, or even longer.

Implications of AGI:

AGI has the potential to revolutionize society, but it also raises significant ethical and existential questions. For example, if AGI surpasses human intelligence, what safeguards will be in place to ensure it benefits humanity rather than causing harm? The development of AGI will require careful consideration of its societal impact, governance, and regulation.

AI in Autonomous Vehicles, Smart Cities, and Healthcare

- **Autonomous Vehicles:**
  Self-driving cars are one of the most high-profile applications of AI in the transportation industry. Companies like **Tesla**, **Waymo**, and **Uber** are working on developing autonomous vehicles that can navigate city streets, highways, and even complex traffic conditions without human intervention. These vehicles rely on a combination of AI technologies, including machine learning, computer vision, and sensor fusion.

  Future Outlook: In the coming years, we can expect autonomous vehicles to become more widespread, improving traffic safety, reducing human error, and transforming the way we think about transportation. However, there are still significant challenges to overcome, including regulatory hurdles, public acceptance, and the need for advanced AI systems to handle complex real-world scenarios.

- **Smart Cities:**

Smart cities are urban areas that use AI and IoT (Internet of Things) technologies to optimize infrastructure, enhance public services, and improve the quality of life for residents. AI can be applied to traffic management, energy distribution, waste management, public safety, and more. For example, AI-powered traffic lights can adjust in real-time to reduce congestion, and sensors can monitor air quality and water usage to optimize city resources.

Future Outlook: As cities around the world adopt smart technologies, we will see more seamless integration of AI into urban planning, making cities more sustainable, efficient, and livable. However, the deployment of AI in public spaces also raises concerns about surveillance, data privacy, and governance, which will need to be addressed.

- **AI in Healthcare:**
AI has the potential to revolutionize healthcare by improving diagnostics, personalizing treatments, and streamlining administrative tasks. AI algorithms can analyze medical data, such as images, genetic information, and electronic health records, to assist doctors in diagnosing diseases

like cancer, heart disease, and neurological disorders. AI can also enable **personalized medicine**, tailoring treatments to an individual's genetic makeup and medical history.

Future Outlook: AI-driven healthcare solutions are expected to reduce costs, improve patient outcomes, and increase access to care, especially in underserved regions. However, challenges around data privacy, algorithmic bias, and regulatory approval will need to be addressed to ensure AI's effectiveness and safety in healthcare.

The Role of AI in Solving Global Challenges

AI is not just transforming industries; it is also being used to tackle some of the world's most pressing global challenges. From climate change to healthcare access, AI has the potential to make a meaningful impact on some of society's greatest problems.

AI for Climate Change

- **Predicting and Mitigating Climate Change:** AI is playing a growing role in addressing **climate change** by helping scientists predict weather patterns, analyze environmental data, and design sustainable solutions. Machine learning algorithms can be used to model climate scenarios, identify sources of pollution, and optimize energy use.

Example: AI-powered systems are being used to analyze satellite data and monitor deforestation, track carbon emissions, and optimize renewable energy usage (e.g., solar and wind power). AI can also help design more energy-efficient buildings and transportation systems, reducing carbon footprints.

- **AI for Renewable Energy:**
  AI can optimize the production, distribution, and consumption of **renewable energy** by predicting energy demand and adjusting supply accordingly. For instance, AI can forecast energy production from solar and wind farms, helping utilities balance the grid and store excess energy for later use.

AI for Healthcare Access
- **Improving Healthcare Access in Underserved Regions:**
  AI has the potential to address disparities in healthcare access, particularly in low-income or rural areas. AI-powered diagnostic tools can be used to provide medical consultations in places where there is a shortage of healthcare

professionals. AI chatbots and virtual assistants can triage symptoms, offer advice, and direct patients to appropriate care.

Example: AI is being used in telemedicine platforms to provide remote consultations in underserved regions. AI-powered diagnostic tools like **IDx-DR** (for detecting diabetic retinopathy) and **PathAI** (for analyzing pathology slides) can provide accurate diagnoses even in areas with limited access to specialists.

- **Drug Discovery and Vaccine Development:**
  AI is speeding up the process of drug discovery by analyzing vast amounts of medical and genetic data to identify potential drug candidates. During the COVID-19 pandemic, AI was used to accelerate vaccine development by analyzing the virus's genetic code and helping scientists identify potential vaccine targets faster than traditional methods.

AI for Education, Poverty Alleviation, and Food Security
- **Education:**
  AI can help increase access to education by providing personalized learning experiences for

students in remote or underserved areas. AI-powered educational tools can adapt to a student's learning pace, provide instant feedback, and offer personalized resources.

- **Poverty Alleviation:**
  AI can assist in poverty alleviation efforts by identifying areas where social programs are most needed, improving resource distribution, and helping organizations design more effective interventions.

- **Food Security:**
  AI is being used to improve agriculture, from precision farming that maximizes crop yields to using machine learning for detecting plant diseases and pests. AI can also help optimize food supply chains, reducing waste and improving access to nutritious food.

Preparing for the AI-Driven Future

As AI continues to shape the future, it's crucial for individuals and organizations to prepare for the changes it will bring. Embracing AI literacy, adapting to new technologies, and understanding the evolving job market will be essential for thriving in an AI-driven world.

The Importance of Learning AI and Staying Adaptable to Future Changes

- **Why Learning AI Matters**:
Understanding AI will be increasingly important for navigating both professional and personal aspects of life. As AI becomes more integrated into various industries, having a basic understanding of how it works will help individuals make informed decisions, engage with AI technologies responsibly, and stay competitive in the workforce.

  AI literacy is not limited to technical fields. Professionals in areas like marketing, healthcare, education, and even the arts will benefit from understanding how AI can enhance their work and improve their decision-making.

- **Staying Adaptable:**
The rapid pace of AI development means that industries and job roles will continuously evolve. Being adaptable and open to learning new skills will be crucial for maintaining career relevance. Continuous upskilling and reskilling will ensure that individuals can take advantage of new opportunities created by AI while staying ahead of potential disruptions.

- **AI Education:**

As AI becomes more embedded in society, educational institutions, governments, and companies will need to prioritize **AI education**. Offering courses on AI fundamentals, machine learning, ethics, and applications can help build a workforce that is prepared for an AI-driven future.

Online platforms like **Coursera, edX**, and **Udacity** offer **AI-related** courses that cater to various skill levels, from beginner to advanced. These platforms enable individuals to learn at their own pace and gain hands-on experience with AI tools and technologies.

Staying Engaged with AI Innovations:
To stay ahead, it's important to follow AI developments and engage with new innovations. Reading AI-related blogs, attending conferences, joining online communities, and experimenting with AI tools will help individuals stay informed and connected to the evolving field of AI.

Conclusion
The future of AI is incredibly exciting, with the potential to revolutionize industries, solve global challenges, and change the way we live and work. As AI continues to advance, we can expect to see the development of **Artificial General Intelligence**, the rise of AI-

powered **autonomous vehicles**, the growth of **smart cities**, and transformative changes in **healthcare** and **climate change** solutions. However, to thrive in an AI-driven future, we must prioritize AI literacy, adaptability, and responsible AI development.

By embracing AI's potential, staying informed about its ethical implications, and preparing for the changes it will bring, we can ensure that AI benefits society as a whole. The AI-driven future is not just something to anticipate—it's something we can actively shape and influence for the betterment of humanity.

Chapter 10

Embracing AI in Your Life

Artificial Intelligence is no longer just a buzzword or a futuristic concept—it is actively shaping the world around us. From automating daily tasks to revolutionizing industries, AI has the potential to improve productivity, creativity, and even solve some of humanity's most pressing challenges. As we've explored throughout this book, AI is a powerful tool that can enhance various aspects of your life, and now it's time to embrace it fully.

In this final chapter, we'll recap the key benefits of using AI, encourage you to continue your journey of exploration, and offer practical tips for integrating AI into your everyday routines.

Final Thoughts on AI

Recap the Benefits of Using AI in Various Aspects of Life

Throughout this book, we've seen how AI can be used in

countless areas to improve both personal and professional life. By now, you should have a solid understanding of the transformative power of AI and its potential to make tasks easier, faster, and more efficient. Here's a quick recap of how AI can benefit you:

- **Enhancing Productivity**: AI tools can automate repetitive tasks, help you manage your time, and provide recommendations to boost your efficiency. Apps like **Trello** for task management and **Zapier** for workflow automation can save you hours of manual work, allowing you to focus on higher-priority tasks.

- **Improving Creativity**: AI can act as a creative partner, helping you brainstorm ideas, generate content, and explore new artistic avenues. Whether you're creating digital art with **DALL-E**, composing music with **Aiva**, or writing articles with **ChatGPT**, AI can amplify your creativity and help you produce high-quality content more efficiently.

- **Solving Problems and Making Decisions**: AI's analytical capabilities can help you make better decisions. For example, AI in personal finance apps like **Mint** and **Acorns** can help you budget, save, and invest wisely. AI-powered tools can also assist in career development, helping you find job opportunities and improve your skills.

- **Improving Health and Wellness**: AI-driven apps like **MyFitnessPal** for fitness tracking and **Headspace** for mindfulness can guide you toward a healthier lifestyle. AI is also transforming healthcare by offering diagnostic tools and personalized health insights that were once only available through medical professionals.

- **Navigating the Future**: As AI continues to evolve, staying informed and adaptable will be crucial for success. AI is not just a tool for today—it will shape the future of work, education, healthcare, and more. Understanding and leveraging AI will be essential for staying competitive in a rapidly changing world.

AI has the potential to enrich many facets of your life, from enhancing personal productivity to opening new creative possibilities. However, its true power lies not just in the tools themselves, but in your ability to embrace and integrate them into your daily routine.

Encourage Readers to Explore and Experiment

with AI Tools

One of the most exciting aspects of AI is that it is accessible to anyone willing to explore it. The AI landscape is rapidly evolving, and new tools are emerging all the time. The more you experiment with these tools, the more you will discover how AI can serve your unique needs and interests.

I encourage you to:

- **Try New AI Tools**: Don't hesitate to experiment with different AI platforms and apps. Whether it's using a writing assistant like **Grammarly** to improve your writing or a creative tool like **DeepArt** to create digital art, the possibilities are endless. The more you experiment, the more you will uncover about what AI can do for you.

- **Stay Curious**: AI is a fast-moving field. Keep exploring different applications, from healthcare and education to entertainment and business. There's always something new to learn and explore. As you grow more comfortable with AI, you may start to see ways to implement it in areas of your life you hadn't initially considered.

- **Join AI Communities**: AI is not just a tool; it's a community of creators, innovators, and thinkers.

Join online communities, participate in discussions, and collaborate with others who are interested in AI. Platforms like **Reddit**, **AI-focused forums**, and **LinkedIn groups** can provide valuable resources and insights from experts and fellow learners.

Next Steps for Beginners

Now that you've explored the fundamentals of AI and its applications, what comes next? Here are some actionable steps to help you continue learning, growing, and integrating AI into your life.

How to Continue Learning About AI After Finishing the Book

The world of AI is vast and constantly evolving. To keep up with the latest trends and technologies, it's important to continue your education and stay engaged with the field. Here are some great ways to continue learning:

- **Online Courses**: There are numerous online platforms that offer AI courses for all skill levels. Here are a few you can explore:

- **Coursera** offers courses like **AI For Everyone** by Andrew Ng and **Machine Learning** by Stanford University, which are excellent for beginners.

- **edX** offers courses from top universities like MIT and Harvard, covering various aspects of AI, from ethics to machine learning.

- **Udacity** offers a comprehensive **AI Nanodegree** program, which is designed for those who want to dive deeper into AI and machine learning.

- **Books and Research Papers**: There are many more books and research papers on AI that can help you deepen your understanding. Some classic titles include **Artificial Intelligence: A Modern Approach** by Stuart Russell and Peter Norvig, and **Deep Learning** by Ian Goodfellow. Reading research papers from journals or preprints (e.g., on **arXiv**) can also keep you informed about cutting-edge AI research.

- **Podcasts and YouTube Channels**: Stay updated with podcasts and YouTube channels dedicated to AI, such as **Lex Fridman Podcast** and **Two Minute Papers**. These platforms offer insights from AI researchers, practitioners, and thought leaders, making complex topics more digestible and relevant to beginners.

- **AI News**: Subscribe to AI news platforms like **VentureBeat AI**, **The Verge AI**, or **MIT Technology** Review to keep up with the latest breakthroughs, tools, and trends in AI.

Tips for Integrating AI into Everyday Routines and Workflows

Integrating AI into your daily life doesn't require a deep technical background. Many AI tools are designed to be user-friendly and accessible, allowing you to enhance your routines and workflows with minimal effort. Here are some practical ways to start:

- **Automate Routine Tasks**: Use AI tools like **Zapier** or **IFTTT** to automate repetitive tasks across your favorite apps. For example, you can set up a workflow that automatically saves email attachments to cloud storage or posts your blog content to social media.

- **Use AI for Personal Productivity**: Leverage AI-powered productivity tools like **RescueTime** for time tracking, **Todoist** for task management, or **Trello** for project organization. These tools can help you stay focused, manage your to-do lists, and optimize your workflow.

- **Enhance Creativity**: If you're a content creator, try using AI tools like **Grammarly** to improve your writing, **ChatGPT** for brainstorming ideas, or **DALL-E** to generate unique images based on your ideas. AI can help you break through creative blocks and produce high-quality content faster.

- **Take Advantage of AI in Communication**: Use AI-driven communication tools such as **Chatbots** for customer service or **Grammarly** for proofreading emails. You can also use **AI translation tools** like **Google** and **Deepl** Translate to communicate with people in other languages, making global interaction easier.

- **Health and Wellness**: Use AI-powered health apps like **MyFitnessPal** for tracking nutrition, **Headspace** for mindfulness, or **Fitbit** for fitness tracking. These tools can help you make healthier decisions and stay on track with your goals.

Conclusion

Artificial Intelligence is a transformative technology that is reshaping the world around us. By embracing AI, you can enhance your productivity, creativity, and even solve complex problems. Whether you're an entrepreneur, artist, student, or simply someone curious about AI, there are endless opportunities to explore.

As you move forward, remember that AI is not a distant concept—it is here, and it's part of the world we live in. By staying curious, continuing to learn, and experimenting with AI tools, you can harness the power of AI to improve your life and work.

The journey doesn't end here. The more you engage with AI, the more you will discover its potential. So, take the next step—continue learning, experimenting, and integrating AI into your life. The future of AI is yours to shape.

Final Message

Congratulations on completing your journey through this book! Now that you have a foundational understanding of AI and how to use it, it's time to continue your learning and exploration. The field of AI is rapidly evolving, and there are countless resources available to deepen your knowledge, connect with other AI enthusiasts, and stay updated on the latest developments.

Your thoughts and experiences are so important! If you connected with this book, I would be deeply grateful if you could share your honest review on Amazon. It helps other members of the 59+ community find resources tailored to their needs.

www.ingramcontent.com/pod-product-compliance
Lightning Source LLC
La Vergne TN
LVHW022352060326
832902LV00022B/4405